ONE-MOVE
CHESS
BY THE
CHAMPIONS

by Bruce Pandolfini

A FIRESIDE BOOK
Published by Simon & Schuster, Inc.
New York

ALSO BY BRUCE PANDOLFINI

Let's Play Chess
Bobby Fischer's Outrageous Chess Moves

Designed by Stanley S. Drate/Folio Graphics Co., Inc.

Manufactured in the United States of America

10 9 8 7 6 5 4 3 2 1

Library of Congress Cataloging in Publication Data

Pandolfini, Bruce.
  One-move chess by the champions.

  "A Fireside book."
  1. Chess players—Biography. 2. Chess—Collections
of games. I. Title.
GV1438.P36   1985   794.1'092'2 [B]   85-14390

ISBN: 978-0-671-60608-4

Acknowledgments

Special thanks must go to Idelle Pandolfini for her careful reading of the text, editing, and helpful suggestions; Chess Master Bruce Alberston for his excellent research and dedicated assistance on the biographies; Carol Ann Caronia for her thoughtful advice; Manhattan Chess Club assistant manager Larry Tamarkin for diagramming the examples; and my friend and personal manager Jonas Green for his creative input, painstaking efforts, and valued guidance, all of which were indispensable to the project. I would like to thank Torrey Paulson, Roane Carey, and Debra Bergman; and Charles Rue Woods for his direction and vision.

Contents

Introduction

While the origins of chess are shrouded in antiquity, the history of the world championship can be traced rather easily. In 1886, J. H. Zukertort and Wilhelm Steinitz slugged it out in the cities of North America (New York, St. Louis, and New Orleans) for the rights to all the marbles. This head-to-head competition was decided in favor of the transplanted Bohemian Steinitz, the first world champion.

Since that time the champion and a challenger have met about every three and a half years. Twenty-nine matches in all, yet there have been only twelve champions. Apparently, no champion readily gives up the throne (with the exception of Bobby Fischer), and all expend superhuman effort to remain at the top as long as possible.

What qualities make a world champion? One attribute stands out: the desire to succeed, to be regarded as the best. This means winning, and in chess terms that translates into one word: Checkmate! It's this instinct for the jugular that separates the champions from other mortals.

Collected in *One-Move Chess by the Champions* are just those positions where the champion scents victory is near and closes in for the kill. The reader is invited to try his hand at finishing off the opponent just as the champion did. Look at the diagrammed position, note the color the champion played (indicated under the diagram), and try to figure out his winning move. If you like, set up the positions on your own board and work out possible solutions. The actual moves the champion played are given at the bottom of the page. Right above the solution you will find a short clue that may help in solving the position. To some extent, these hints are enigmatic riddles, so use them at your own peril. As a final feature, each problem is evaluated in terms of difficulty, from 1 to 5, with 5 being the most difficult. These values will appear in the shaded area on the top right of each page. So, get ready to test your skill with that of the world champions, the best chessplayers the game has ever seen.

About Algebraic Notation

Algebraic notation is the clearest way to describe chess moves, using letters **a** to **h** and numbers **1** to **8**. It's also the officially recognized notational system of both the world and U.S. chess federations (FIDE and USCF, respectively).

The chessboard itself is an 8-by-8 grid, with vertical rows called *files* and horizontal rows called *ranks.* Letters signify files, numbers designate ranks.

Each square is named by its intersecting letter and number as in diagram A. In diagram B, White's King occupies b6; White's Bishops d7 and e7; and Black's King b8. All squares are always named from White's point of view.

Symbols you should know

K means King
Q means Queen
R means Rook
B means Bishop
N means Knight (so as not to confuse with the King)

Pawns are not symbolized (they are named by the letter of the file occupied—the pawn on the b-file is the b-pawn)

x means captures
+ means check
0-0 means castles Kingside
0-0-0 means castles Queenside
! means very good move
!! means brilliant move
? means questionable move
?? means blunder
1. means White's first move
1 . . . means Black's first move
(1-0) means White wins
(0-1) means Black wins

5

Reading the Line Score of a Game

Consider diagram B. White to play could mate in two moves and it would be written this way:

1. Bd6 + Ka8 2. Bc6 mate.

1. Bd6 + means that White's first move was Bishop to d6 check.

Ka8 means that Black's first move was King to a8.

2. Bc6 mate means that White's second move was Bishop to c6 checkmate.

Note that the number of the move is written only once, appearing just before White's play. For the examples in the book, the winning move is given in boldface type, while other moves and possibilities appear in regular type.

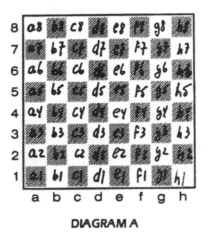

DIAGRAM A

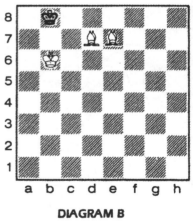

DIAGRAM B

6

About the Twelve World Champions

Wilhelm Steinitz (1836-1900)

WORLD CHAMPION 1866-94
Austria

Wilhelm Steinitz was generally acknowledged as the world's top player from 1866, when he won an historic match from Germany's Adolph Anderssen, to 1886, when he was declared the first official world champion by triumphing in a twenty-game showdown over Poland's Johann Hermann Zukertort. When the Prague-born Steinitz was finally dethroned in 1894 at the age of fifty-eight by the younger Emanuel Lasker, it marked the first time he had ever lost a match.

Steinitz's forty-year career revolutionized the nature of the game from a pleasant amateur's pastime into the robust mental sport of the victory-oriented professional. Earlier chess was romantic, with slashing gambits, headlong sacrifices, and unfathomable risks. Steinitz saw in it a more integrated purpose. A tenacious and resourceful defender, the little man "who taught us how to play chess" understood the inherent possibilities in every position. No position could be conquered unless its balance was already disturbed. This he attempted to do by accumulating small advantages, each seemingly insignificant by itself, but collectively adding up to a decisive superiority. His attacks were painstakingly built on a grand scale, and when the blow came the opponent's position was shattered beyond escape. These ideas formed the basis for his theory of position play, the trademark of the modern grandmaster. As the bridge from romantic to classical chess developed (1885 to 1914), Steinitz singlehandedly laid the foundations of contemporary chess science.

Steinitz vs. an amateur

VIENNA 1861

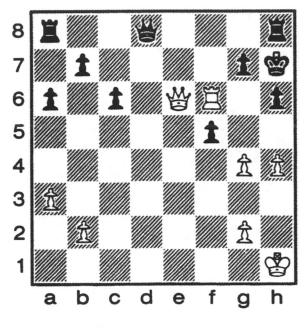

WHITE TO MOVE

KEY: An open and shut place

SOLUTION: Steinitz dynamited his entry by **1. Rxh6 + !** gxh6, and closed in with 2. Qf7—an epaulette mate, where the losing King is blocked to the right and left by his own men.

Rainer vs. Steinitz

VIENNA 1860

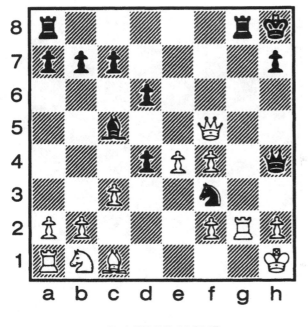

BLACK TO MOVE

KEY: Divert and conquer

SOLUTION: There's an Arabian mate at g1 (the Rook checks supported by the Knight) after **1 . . . Qxh2 + !** 2. Rxh2 Rg1.

Steinitz vs. Hodges

NEW YORK 1891

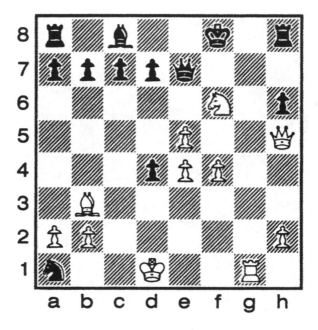

a b c d e f g h

WHITE TO MOVE

KEY: Ripoff

SOLUTION: The unexpected brutal capture **1. Qxh6 + !** wins, for 1 . . . Rxh6 2. Rg8 is mate, as is 1 . . .Qg7 2. Qxg7.

Steinitz vs. Golmayo

HAVANA 1898

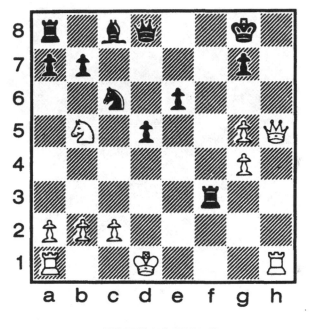

WHITE TO MOVE

KEY: Keep your traps shut

SOLUTION: 1. g6! sealed Black's fate. If 1 . . . Kf8, then 2. Qh8+ Ke7 3. Qxg7+ Ke8 4. Rh8+ Rf8 5. Rxf8 mate. Steinitz prepared this line by bringing his Knight to b5 on the previous move, depriving the enemy King of the escape square d6.

Steinitz vs. an amateur

VIENNA 1861

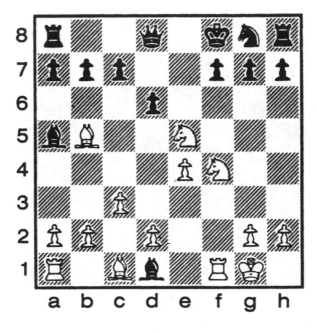

WHITE TO MOVE

KEY: A gift horse in the mate

SOLUTION: 1. Nf-g6 + hxg6 2. Nxg6 mate. Curiously, sacrificing initially on g6 with the other Knight also mates.

Steinitz vs. Paulsen

BADEN-BADEN 1870

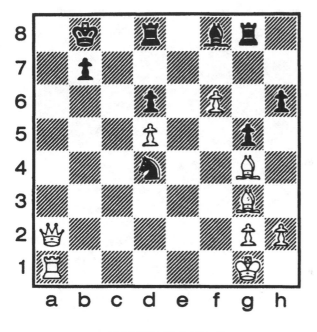

WHITE TO MOVE

KEY: Seventh heaven

SOLUTION: 1. Qa7 + (better than a check on the 8th rank because it creates a pin on the b-pawn) Kc7 2. Rc1 + Nc6 3. Rxc6 mate.

Hampe vs. Steinitz

VIENNA 1859

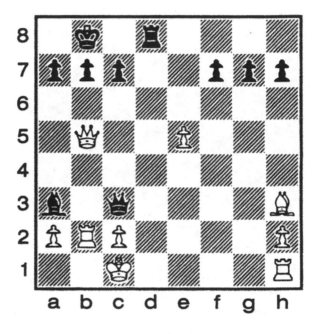

BLACK TO MOVE

KEY: Turning point

SOLUTION: Black squashes White's b7 mate threat and turns it around: **1 . . . Qd2+** 2. Kb1 Qd1+ and mate next move.

Steinitz vs. Pihal

VIENNA 1862

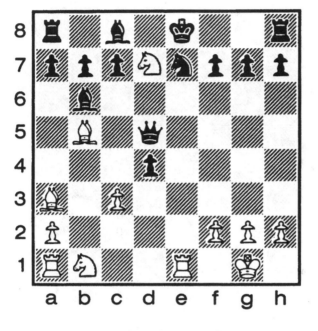

WHITE TO MOVE

KEY: The irreverent Bishops

SOLUTION: Black forgot about White's two Bishops. It was mate after **1. Nf6+ +!** (double check) 1 . . . Kd8 (or 1 . . . Kf8) 2. Bxe7.

Steinitz vs. Tchigorin

HAVANA 1892

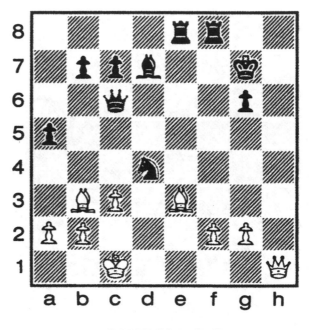

WHITE TO MOVE

KEY: Woman's work

SOLUTION: The Queen conducts the attack with **1. Qh6 + !** Kf6 2. Qh4 +, leading to a quick mate. If 2 . . . g5, then 3. Qxg5 mate. Or if 2 . . . Kf5 (or 2 . . . Ke5 3. Qxd4 + Kf5 4. Qf4 mate), then 3. Qf4 mate. And if 2 . . . Kg7, then 3. Bh6 + Kh8 (or Kh7) 4. Bxf8 discovered mate.

Emanuel Lasker (1868-1941)

World Champion 1894-1921
Germany

A follower of the first world champion, Lasker held the title from his 1894 victory over Steinitz to his 1921 defeat at the hands of Cuban whirlwind José Raoul Capablanca. (Citing exhaustion, Lasker actually resigned the match after a mere fourteen games.) From his first tournament success (1890) in his own Berlin to his final participation at Nottingham (1936), he proved to be a ferocious competitor. Twice (at St. Petersburg 1914 and New York 1924) he won outstanding tournaments ahead of his two great rivals, Capablanca and Alekhine. Perhaps the real test of his fighting spirit was his third-place finish at Moscow in 1935. He was sixty-seven years old!

Emanuel Lasker was many chess types rolled into one: tactician, positional player, defensive genius, psychologist, and fighter. He also may have been the greatest endgame player of all time. His rivals couldn't unlock the key to his style, attributing his success to his smelly cigars, Lady Luck, or contracts with Satan. Not theories but only strong moves interested him. His forte was hand-to-hand fighting where a momentary slackening of attention could prove disastrous. A strong-nerved player, he took calculated risks or made inferior moves in order to steer the play along paths certain to discomfit his opponent. He was a razor's edge grappler whose conduct in critically important games had monumental resonance. He finished his career with the second-highest winning percentage of all the champions.

Lasker vs. Gunsberg

HASTINGS 1895

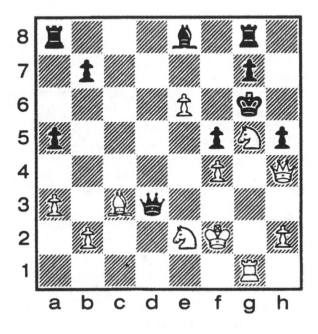

WHITE TO MOVE

KEY: Jumping to a conclusion

SOLUTION: The Knight's leap **1. Nf7 + !** uncovers a lurking check. Since 1 . . . Kh7 allows 2. Qxh5 mate, Black resigned.

Tartakover vs. Lasker

NEW YORK 1924

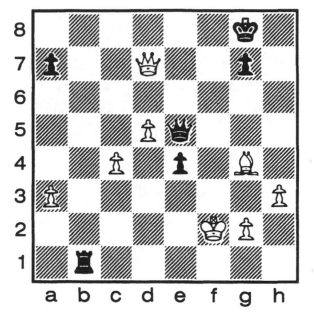

BLACK TO MOVE

KEY: When push comes to shove

SOLUTION: White was gradually forced to the back rank with **1 . . . e3 + !** 2. Ke2 Rb2 + 3. Ke1 Qc3 + 4. Kf1 Qc1 + and white resigned, for 5. Bd1 Qxd1 is mate. If 2. Kf3 Rf1 + 3. Ke2 Rf2 + 4. Ke1 (4. Kd3 Rd2 mate), then 4 . . . Qc3 + and 5 . . . Qd2 mate.

2

Lasker vs. Steinitz
MOSCOW 1896

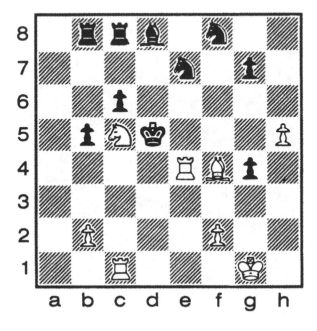

WHITE TO MOVE

KEY: Direct access

SOLUTION: Try mate in two straightforward, uninterruptible checks: **1. Rd1 +** Kxc5 2. Be3.

Porges vs. Lasker

NUREMBERG 1896

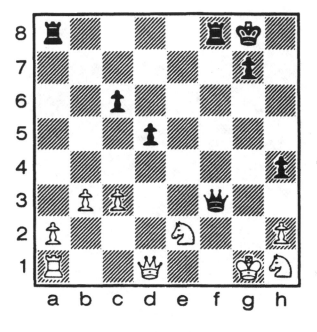

BLACK TO MOVE

KEY: A little pawn is a dangerous thing

SOLUTION: After **1 . . . Qe3+** 2. Kg2, Black's h-pawn conquers with 2 . . . h3 mate! Neat and simple.

Allies vs. Lasker

PHILADELPHIA 1907

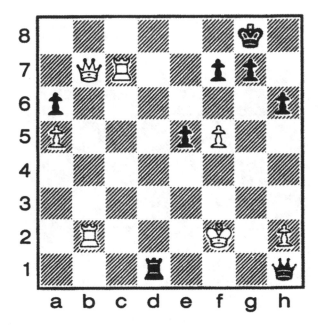

BLACK TO MOVE

KEY: The third man

SOLUTION: Black progresses with major pieces, but in the end wins with the aid of a pawn: 1 . . . Qf1+ 2. Ke3 (or 2. Kg3 Rd3+ 3. Kg4 Qh3 mate) 2 . . . Rd3+ 3. Ke4 Qf3+ 4. Kxe5 Qe3+ 5. Qe4 f6+ I and mate next move.

Lasker vs. Hennerberger

ZURICH 1934

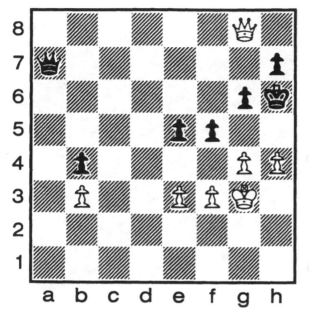

WHITE TO MOVE

KEY: Ladies first

SOLUTION: White starts with a Queen check and waits a move before pushing his pawn. **1. Qf8+** wins, for 1 . . . Qg7 2. g5+ soon mates (2 . . . Kh5 3. Qxg7 threatening 4. Qh6).

Fillacik vs. Lasker

ZAGREB 1924

BLACK TO MOVE

KEY: Close your encounters

SOLUTION: Lasker tightens the cordon with **1 . . . Rg3!**, planning 2 . . . g6 mate. All defenses falter, including a Rook sack (2. Rxe6 g6+ 3. Rxg6 Rxg6), when the Knight will mate at g7 or g3.

Lasker vs. Schiffers

NUREMBERG 1896

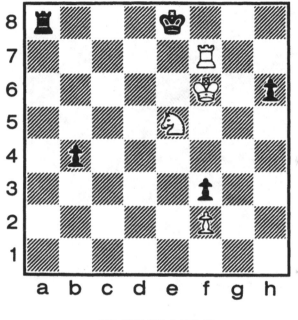

WHITE TO MOVE

KEY: Win in a walkover

SOLUTION: Mate results after **1. Re7 + !**. If 1 . . . Kd8, then 2. Nf7 + Kc8 3. Nd6 + Kd8 (3 . . . Kb8 is answered by 4. Rb7 mate) 4. Ke6 and Rd7 mate is coming. If 1 . . . Kf8, then 2. Ng6 + Kg8 3. Rg7 mate.

Pillsbury vs. Lasker

ST. PETERSBURG 1895-96

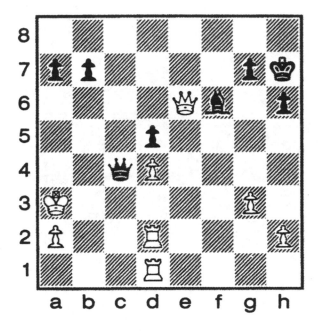

BLACK TO MOVE

KEY: Crossfire

SOLUTION: A Lasker classic: 1 . . . Qc3+ 2. Ka4 b5+! 3. Kxb5 Qc4+ 4. Ka5 Bd8+, and Black criss-cross mates next move.

José Raoul Capablanca (1888-1942)

WORLD CHAMPION 1921-27
Cuba

The "Invincible" Capablanca was one of the greatest natural chess talents of all time. It is said that he learned the moves at the age of four merely by watching his father play. For eight years he didn't lose a single match or tournament game, and when he died after suffering a stroke at the Manhattan Chess Club in 1942, he had lost no more than thirty-seven serious games in his lifetime, far fewer than any other top player.

Coordination and harmony were the intrinsic gifts of this Mozartian wizard of the chess world. He played rapidly and easily, as if born to the art. Capablanca exhibited no false steps, no misreadings of the position, somehow landing his pieces on just the right squares. He handled attacking, combinative chess with the best, but preferred clear, solid positions, relying on a superb technique and an extraordinary feel for the endgame. These skills were already in evidence when at twelve Capablanca won the championship of Cuba in a match with Juan Corzo.

With his great abilities and striking good looks, Capablanca was idolized both in and out of the chess world. In a major magazine's poll in the 1920s, he was ranked as the world's third most handsome man, right behind Rudolf Valentino and Ramon Novarro. Cecil B. DeMille even brought him to Hollywood, where he planned to make him a star. But it's as a chessplayer that he will be remembered, one of the truly best.

Capablanca vs. Menchik

MARGATE 1935

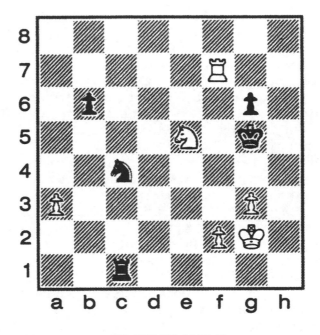

WHITE TO MOVE

KEY: Horsing around

SOLUTION: 1. f4 + ! wins, for 1 . . . Kh6 (1 . . . Kh5 2. Rh7 mate) 2. Ng4+ Kh5 3. Nf6+ (a nifty pirouette) Kh6 4. Rh7 mate.

Capablanca vs. Vassaux

BUENOS AIRES 1939

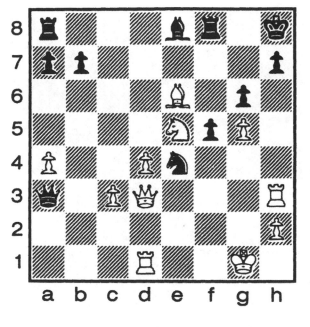

WHITE TO MOVE

KEY: The unveiling

SOLUTION: 1. Rxh7 + ! Kxh7 2. Qh3 + Kg7 3. Qh6, and the exposed King is mated.

Capablanca vs. Stahr

CHICAGO 1915

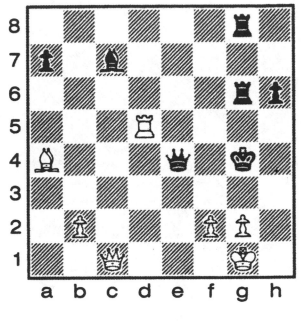

WHITE TO MOVE

KEY: End-to-end play

SOLUTION: The Bishop is transported from the middle of the a-file to the center of the 1st rank and the mate is given at the hub of the h-file: **1. Bd1 + !** Kh4 2. Rh5 mate.

Capablanca vs. Maddock

NEW YORK 1922

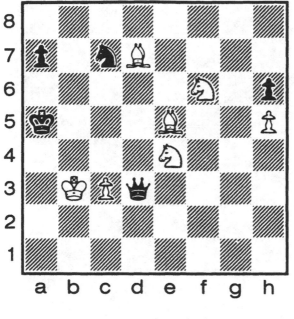

WHITE TO MOVE

KEY: The gang of four

SOLUTION: 1. Bxc7 + Ka6 2. Nc5 mate. White's four minor pieces have ferociously outplayed Black's Queen and Knight.

Capablanca vs. Carter
ST. LOUIS 1909

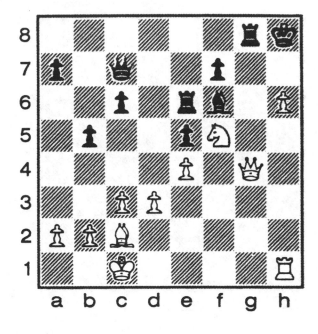

WHITE TO MOVE

KEY: Queen for a play

SOLUTION: White's sudden hara-kiri nosedive **1. Qg7 + !** curtailed matters considerably. If Black had continued 1 . . . Bxg7, he would have met 2. hxg7 double check and mate. And if 1 . . . Rxg7, then 2. hxg7 + Kg8 loses to 3. Rh8 mate.

Capablanca vs. Raubitschek

NEW YORK 1906

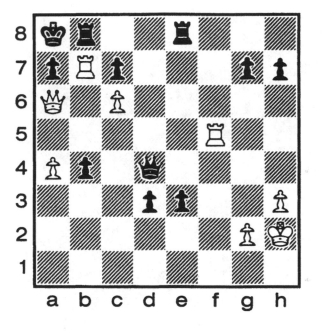

WHITE TO MOVE

KEY: Rooked again

SOLUTION: 1. Rxa7 + !! Qxa7 **2. Ra5!,** and it's mate next move. White's quiet Rook move scores.

An amateur vs. Capablanca

NEW YORK 1911

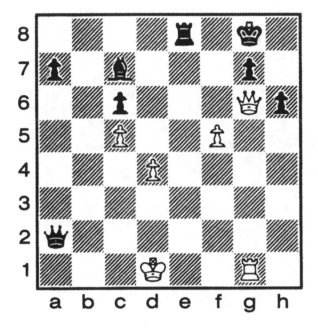

BLACK TO MOVE

KEY: Three for the seesaw

SOLUTION: White's attack totters as Black's trio teeters mate the other way: **1 . . . Qb1 + !** 2. Kd2 Ba5 mate.

Capablanca vs. Jaffe

NEW YORK 1910

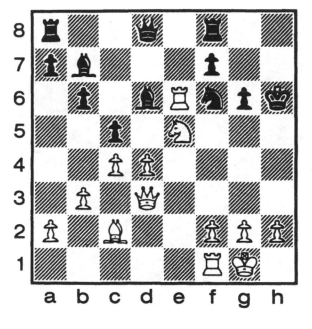

WHITE TO MOVE

KEY: Underpinning undermined

SOLUTION: The King is dead after **1. Nxf7 + !**, when the support for g6 is knocked out. White then plays 2. Qxg6.

Bogolubov vs. Capablanca

BAD KISSINGEN 1928

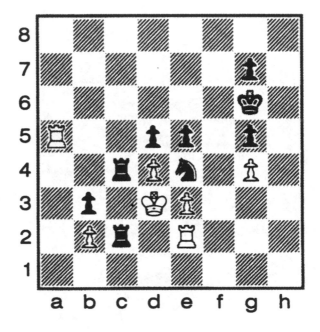

BLACK TO MOVE

KEY: A pawn in the game

SOLUTION: Black's e-pawn administers the mate: 1 . . . **Nc5+** (also good is 1 . . . Nf2+) 2. dxc5 e4 mate!

Alexander Alekhine (1892-1946)

WORLD CHAMPION 1927-35, 1937-46
Russia

The man who defeated the Invincible Capablanca in 1927 was a Russian emigre named Alexander Alekhine. Devoted to the game, Alekhine usually spent at least ten hours a day studying chess. He had few friends and was not admired as a person, though his great chess talent was appreciated worldwide. He is the only champion to die while still in possession of the title.

Creatively, he managed the difficult fusion of fantasy and practicality like no player before or since. His restless imagination reveled in complexity, but even in very simple positions he unearthed resources no one else dreamed of. His games were a fountain of opening novelties and what Bobby Fischer deemed "outrageous, unprecedented" conceptions. In his writings, Alekhine delighted in explaining how his preposterous ideas were really rooted in the logic of the position. At the board Alekhine was a psychologically menacing personality, smoking, twirling his hair, glaring down his opponent, sometimes circling the table like a beast of prey. Yet to many, his collected games are masterpieces that elevated chess to the highest level of intellectual and aesthetic attainment.

Alekhine vs. Fletcher

LONDON 1928

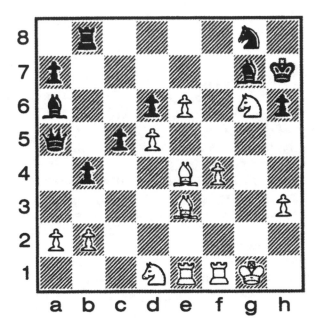

WHITE TO MOVE

KEY: He can run but he can't hide

SOLUTION: After **1. Ne5 + !**, Black's King can flee to the corner but 2. Nf7 is still mate.

Alekhine vs.Steiner
DRESDEN 1928

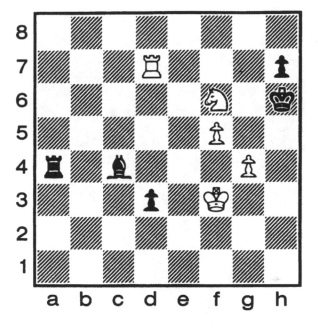

WHITE TO MOVE

KEY: All in the family

SOLUTION: The entire White clan is needed for this two-move mate: **1. Rxh7 +** Kg5 2. Ne4 mate.

Bogolubov vs. Alekhine

GERMANY—HOLLAND 1929

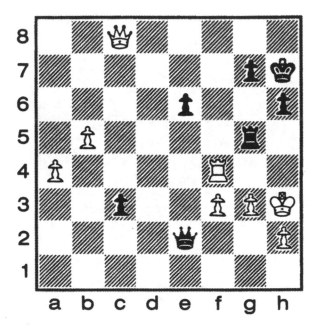

BLACK TO MOVE

KEY: She drives him up the wall

SOLUTION: The King is henpecked to submission after **1 . . . Qf1+** 2. Kh4 Rh5 + ! 3. Kxh5 (3. Kg4 Qh3 mate) 3 . . . Qh3 + 4. Rh4 Qf5 mate (or 4 . . . g6 mate).

Blumenfeld vs. Alekhine

MOSCOW 1908

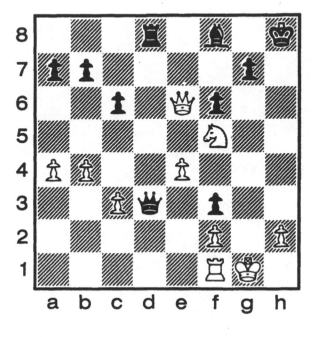

BLACK TO MOVE

KEY: An uncoverup

SOLUTION: Black strips the back rank and mates with **1 . . . Qxf1 + ! 2. Kxf1 Rd1.**

Alekhine vs. Lasker

ZURICH 1934

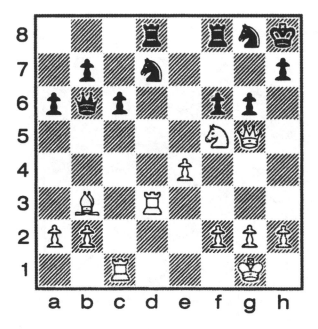

WHITE TO MOVE

KEY: Expropriate appropriately

SOLUTION: The game was seized with **1. Qxg6!!,** when defending against the mate threat at g7 by 1 . . . hxg6 allows 2. Rh3+ Nh6 3. Rxh6 mate.

Alekhine vs. Supico

TENERIFE 1945

WHITE TO MOVE

KEY: The ultimate sacrifice?

SOLUTION: Black is toppled after **1. Qg6!!**, when White's Queen cannot be accepted with impunity. For example, if 1 . . . hxg6, then 2. Rh3 mate. Or if 1 . . . fxg6, then 2. Nxg6+ hxg6 3. Rh3 mate. Finally, if 1 . . . Rg8 (to guard against 2. Qxg7 mate), then 2. Qxh7+ ! Kxh7 3. Rh3, and it's mate again!

Alekhine vs. an amateur

RUSSIA 1910?

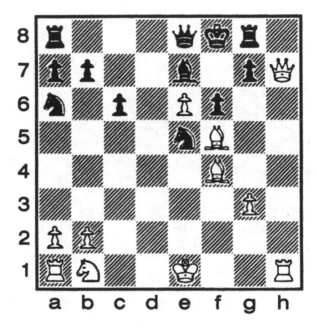

WHITE TO MOVE

KEY: Forced entry

SOLUTION: White broke into Black's sanctuary with **1. Qxg7 + !!**. It's mate after both 1 . . . Rxg7 2. Rh8 + Rg8 3. Bh6 and 1 . . . Kxg7 2. Bh6 + Kh8 3. Bf8 + Qh5 4. Rxh5.

Alekhine vs. Maroczy

BLED 1931

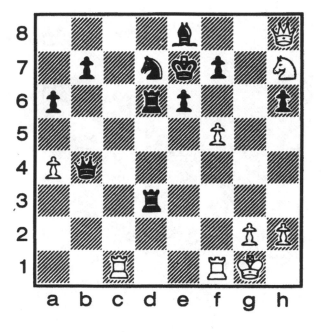

WHITE TO MOVE

KEY: A regular checkup

SOLUTION: Pretty mates result from the pawn advance **1. f6 + !.** If 1 . . . Nxf6, then 2. Qxf6 + Kd7 3. Nf8 mate. Or if 1 . . . Kd8, then 2. Qxe8 + ! Kxe8 3. Rc8 mate.

Alekhine vs. Reshevsky

KEMERI 1937

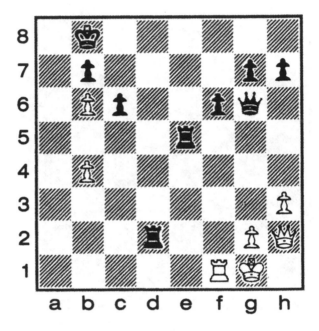

WHITE TO MOVE

KEY: Can opener

SOLUTION: It's mate in all variations after **1. Qxe5 + !!**: 1 . . .
fxe5 2. Rf8 + and mate in two moves; 1 . . . Kc8 2. Qc7 mate; 1
. . . Ka8 2. Ra1 + and mate next move.

Max Euwe (1901-81)

WORLD CHAMPION 1935-37
Holland

Dr. Euwe was a dark horse when he faced world champion Alekhine in 1935. Few critics gave him a chance against the awesome Russian, but he managed to wrest away the title by a single game. In 1937, he lost the title back to Alekhine in a return match, but for years he was still considered one of the game's strongest players. He was the only world champion to also serve as president of the world chess federation (FIDE), a position he held from 1970 to 1978.

A true Renaissance man with a variety of interests, Dr. Euwe had to compartmentalize his time: so much for family, work, chess, and so on. He approached chess in a similarly methodical manner, breaking it down into openings, tactics, positional play, and endgames. Positions were collected and crammed into his notebooks, analyzed and sifted, and became the basis for the excellent books he wrote, which were always stimulating. Stylistically he was a master of lively positions with pieces in conflict over the whole board. The similarity to Fischer's technique is unmistakable, with emphasis on opening preparations and tactical calculation. He will be remembered for his scholarly work, his gentlemanliness, and his sporting qualities.

Euwe vs. Loman
HOLLAND 1923

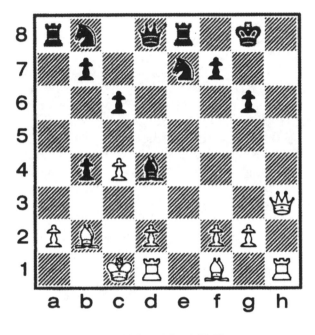

WHITE TO MOVE

KEY: The monkey in the middle

SOLUTION: Thanks to White's X-ray attack on h8, he mates by **1. Qh8 + !** Bxh8 2. Rxh8 mate.

Euwe vs. Blek

AMSTERDAM 1928

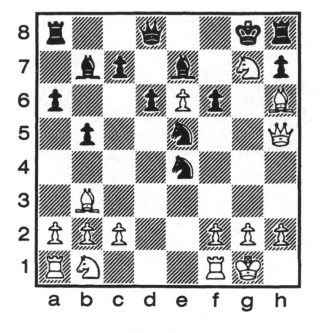

WHITE TO MOVE

KEY: The lady's not a tramp

SOLUTION: The Queen sacrifice **1. Qf7 + !!** wins at once, for
1 . . . Nxf7 2. exf7 + Kf8 3. Nf5 (or 3 Ne8) is discovered mate.

Euwe vs. Speyer
HOLLAND 1924

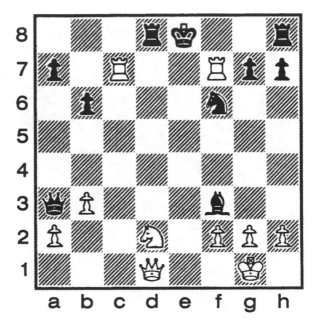

WHITE TO MOVE

KEY: She picks up the check

SOLUTION: The Queen shift **1. Qe1 + !** inevitably mates, for White captures any piece interposed at e4 with his Knight, threatening an unanswerable discovered check.

Szabo vs. Euwe

GRONINGEN 1946

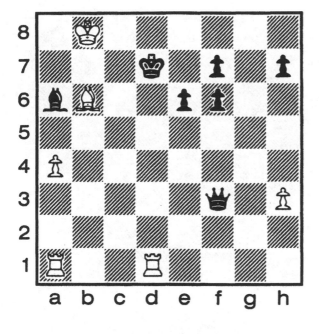

BLACK TO MOVE

KEY: Appearances sure are deceiving

SOLUTION: Black's in check, but by withdrawing his King to the back row **1 . . . Ke8**, he's the one who menaces mate at b7. If White tries 2. Kc7, for example, then 2 . . . Qb7+ 3. Kd6 Qxb6 mates anyway.

Oskam vs. Euwe

AMSTERDAM 1920

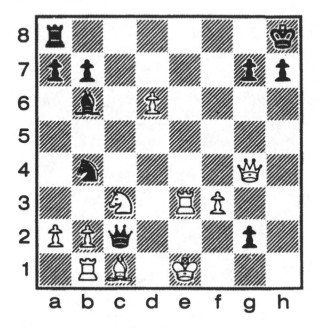

BLACK TO MOVE

KEY: A three-bagger

SOLUTION: After 1 . . . Nd3 +, White gets mated next move
(2. Rxd3 Bf2), when all three attackers in Black's mating force
occupy the 2nd rank.

Euwe vs. Westerman

AMSTERDAM 1933

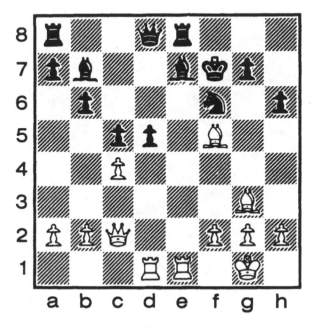

WHITE TO MOVE

KEY: The Bishop makes a play for the Queen?

SOLUTION: After the clearance check **1. Be6 + !** Kf8, White's
Queen enters the fray by 2. Qg6, soon imposing mate at f7.

Euwe vs. Lohr

AMSTERDAM 1923

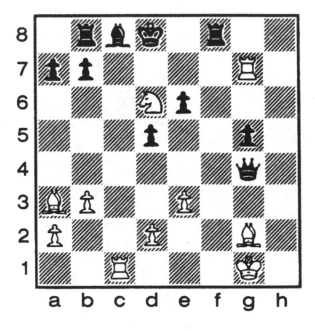

WHITE TO MOVE

KEY: Bottoms up

SOLUTION: Jetting his Rook from the 1st rank to the 8th, White forces mate in three: **1. Rxc8+** Rxc8 2. Nxb7+ Ke8 3. Re7 mate.

Kleefstra vs. Euwe

AMSTERDAM 1933

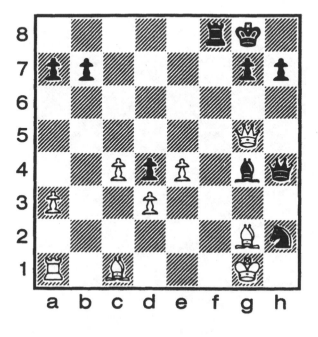

BLACK TO MOVE

KEY: No castle keep

SOLUTION: After the Rook sack **1 . . . Rf1 + I** 2. Bxf1 Qg3 +,
Black quickly garners the enemy King. If 3. Kh1, then 3 . . .
Bf3 + 4. Bg2 Bxg2 + 5. Kg1 Nf3 mate. Or if 3. Bg2, then 3 . . .
Nf3 + 4. Kf1 (4. Kh1 Qh2 mate) Qe1 mate.

Euwe vs. Thomas
HASTINGS 1934-35

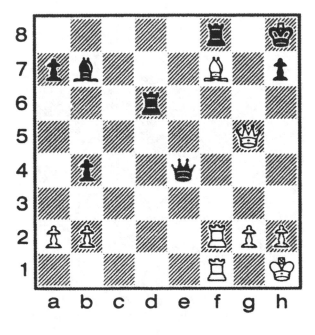

WHITE TO MOVE

KEY: Cut two pieces

SOLUTION: 1. Bd5!! and Black resigned. For example, if 1 . . . Rxf2, then 2. Qg8 mate. Otherwise, White checks at f8 and shortly mates.

Mikhail Botvinnik (1911-)

WORLD CHAMPION 1948-57, 1958-60, 1961-63
Soviet Union

Mikhail Botvinnik rose to the world championship by winning the great 1948 Hague-Moscow tournament, an event to reestablish the title Alekhine held at his death. But by this time he was already regarded as the game's best player, so his success was not unexpected. He is the only man to regain the title twice, from Smyslov in 1958 and Tal in 1961. Since losing the championship, he has devoted his time to computer chess, espousing the view that someday there will emerge a programmed world champion!

His highly individualistic chess style is hardly a reflection of Soviet collectivism, but he is nevertheless called "Mr. Soviet Chess." He certainly has had an inspiring effect on the game in his home country. A profound thinker along Steinitz's model, Botvinnik excelled in complex strategical positions requiring dynamic breakthroughs. His opening preparation was awesome: whole new systems were meticulously developed and charted well into the middle game. This, together with a superb endgame skill, defines a player who was at home in all phases of the game. In recent years, he has also shone as a teacher, and his best-known pupil is Gary Kasparov!

Goglidze vs. Botvinnik

MOSCOW 1935

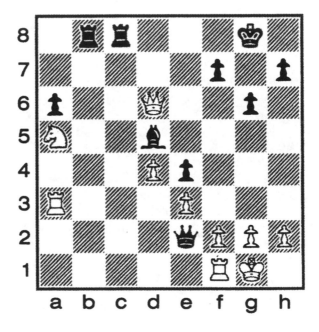

BLACK TO MOVE

KEY: Rook-ends

SOLUTION: The Rooks do the job after 1 . . . Qxf1 + ! 2. Kxf1 Rc1 + 3. Ke2 Rb2, with the mate delivered along the 2nd rank.

Botvinnik vs. Yudovich

MOSCOW 1933

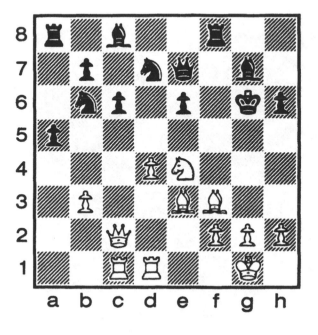

WHITE TO MOVE

KEY: Hold your horses

SOLUTION: Instead of giving an immediate check by moving the Knight, Botvinnik interpolated **1. Bh5 + !!**, which leads to a forced mate. If 1 . . . Kxh5, then 2. Ng3+ followed by 3. Qe4 mates. And the retreat 1 . . . Kh7 loses to 2. Nf6+ + (double check) Kh8 3. Qh7 mate, so Black gave up.

3

Rabinovich vs. Botvinnik
LENINGRAD 1926

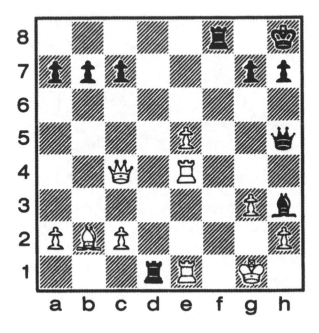

BLACK TO MOVE

KEY: The bottom line

SOLUTION: The incursion **1 . . . Qf3!** leads to mate, there being no way to cover g2. If 2. Qe2 (or 2. Re2), then Black's back-rank Rook deflects the defense with 2 . . . Rxe1 +, and it's mate next move.

60

Bondarevsky vs. Botvinnik

MOSCOW 1941

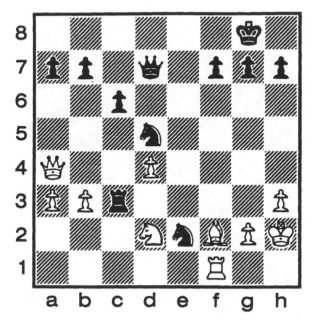

BLACK TO MOVE

KEY: Pawn shopping

SOLUTION: Black's attack focuses on the h-pawn from afar 1
. . . **Rxh3 + !**. 2. gxh3 Nd-f4 is the tactical execution, and
White can't prevent Qxh3 mate.

Botvinnik vs. Goglidze

MOSCOW 1931

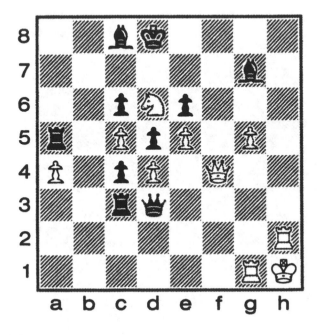

WHITE TO MOVE

KEY: Between a Rook and a hard-to-guard-place

SOLUTION: By decoying Black's Bishop from defending f8 with a Rook sacrifice **1. Rh8 + !**, White's Queen can exploit the weakened last row: 1 . . . Bxh8 2. Qf8 + Kd7 3. Qxc8 + Ke7 4. Qe8 mate (also good is 3. Qe8 + Kc7 4. Qxc8 mate).

Botvinnik vs. Bondarevsky

MOSCOW 1945

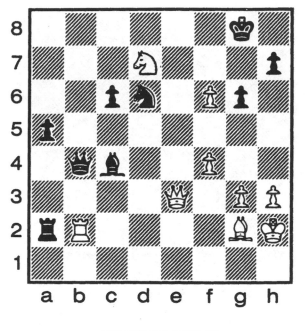

WHITE TO MOVE

KEY: Haste makes waste

SOLUTION: White could take Black's Queen and then mate, but a faster way is **1. Qe7!**, and Black is quickly mated no matter what he does. Either he blocks g7 with his Bishop 1 . . . Bf7 and allows 2. Qf8 mate, or he moves his Knight (say, 1 . . . Nf5) and falls by 2. Qe8+ Qf8 3. Qxf8 mate.

Botvinnik vs. Yudovich

MOSCOW 1935

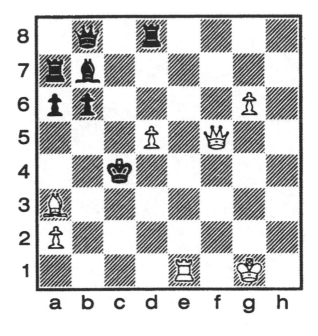

WHITE TO MOVE

KEY: Three strikes and you're out

SOLUTION: White's Queen and Bishop throw three straight curves: **1. Qe4+!** (all other first moves take longer to effect the mate) 1 . . . Kc3 (1 . . . Kb5 allows 2. Qb4 mate) 2. Bb4+ Kb2 3. Qb1 mate.

Dubinin vs. Botvinnik

MOSCOW 1958

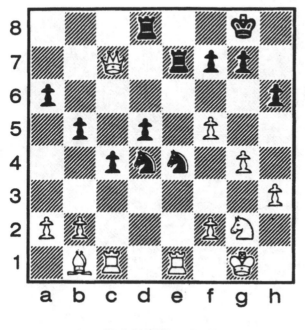

BLACK TO MOVE

KEY: Changing horses in midstream

SOLUTION: Black takes the reins with **1 . . . Nf3 +**. If 2. Kf1, then 2 . . . Ne-d2 mate. And if 2. Kh1, then again the other Knight lowers the boom 2 . . . Nxf2 mate.

Botvinnik vs. Keres

HAGUE 1948

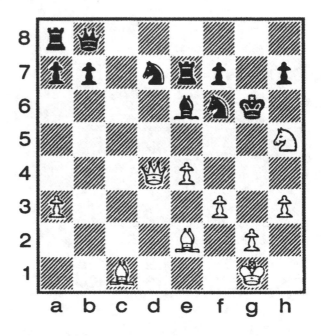

WHITE TO MOVE

KEY: Nice and easy does it

SOLUTION: The simple shift **1. Qe3!** induced Keres to resign, for he had no adequate defense to the tandem mate threats at g5 and h6.

Vassily Smyslov (1921-)

WORLD CHAMPION 1957-58
Soviet Union

The seventh world chess champion, Vassily Smyslov, learned how to play in his father's library at the age of six. He developed rapidly, and was eventually recognized as the second greatest Soviet player in the 1940s, right behind Botvinnik. He played three world championship matches with Botvinnik, drawing in 1954, winning in 1957, and losing in 1958. After 69 match games with the great Botvinnik, Smyslov stood one point ahead. As late as 1983, he was still competing in the world championship cycle! (Shades of Lasker.)

Harmony, however, is the byword that places Smyslov in Capablanca's Club. A finished master of all phases of the game, Smyslov is one of the truly great opening innovators in chess history, with a superbly flowing, logically conducted middle game and an artistry in the endgame second to none. The complications he sought as a youth yielded to a more temperate, controlled technical style as he mobilized his assault on Botvinnik's crown. Little could be left to chance if his outstanding gifts were to be realized. This might have led to dry, uninteresting games, but connoisseurs regard his as endlessly rewarding and instructive.

Smyslov vs. Botvinnik

MOSCOW 1958

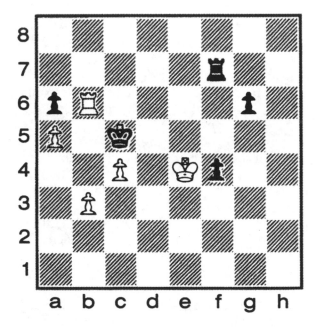

WHITE TO MOVE

KEY: The lion's den

SOLUTION: Botvinnik, having rashly entered White's lair, is caught in a mating trap after **1. Kd3!**, when a check at b4 looms large.

Smyslov vs. Filip

VIENNA 1957

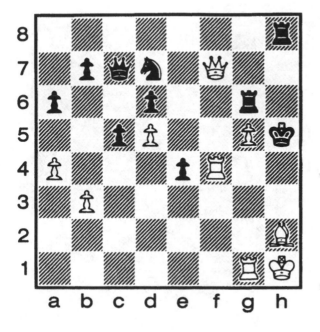

WHITE TO MOVE

KEY: The sure thing

SOLUTION: White has a few powerful tries, but the most certain is **1. Qf5!**, which forces Black's resignation because of the overwhelming mate threats at g4 and h3. Black's best try is 1 . . . Rg7 (or Rg-g8), but he's still mated after 2. Rh4 + ! Kxh4 3. Qg4.

Fuderer vs. Smyslov
ZAGREB 1955

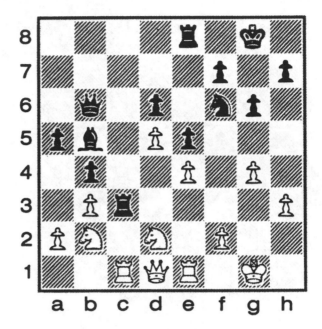

BLACK TO MOVE

KEY: Into the valley of death

SOLUTION: Smyslov sallied **1. . . . Rg3 + !**, and the pinned f-pawn is unable to capture the Rook. After 2. Kh1 Qxf2, Black will mate at either g2 or h3.

Smyslov vs. Zak

MOSCOW 1938

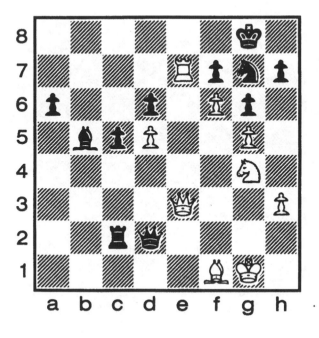

WHITE TO MOVE

KEY: Knight rider

SOLUTION: White's Knight rides roughshod with **1. Nh6+** Kh8 (1 . . . Kf8 2. Rxf7 mate) 2. Nxf7+ Kg8 3. Nh6+ Kh8 (or 3 . . . Kf8) 4. fxg7 mate.

Smyslov vs. Gereben

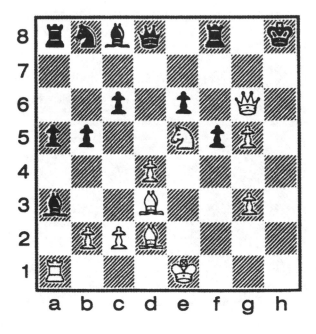

WHITE TO MOVE

KEY: Advance man

SOLUTION: White moves up in the world with **1. Ke2!**, when mate by the Rook along the h-file is certain.

Smyslov vs. Hubner

VELDEN 1983

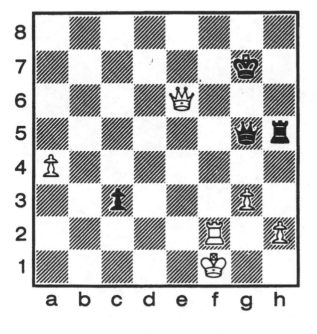

WHITE TO MOVE

KEY: On the up and up

SOLUTION: First the Rook invades **1. Rf7 +** Kh8 (Black thus keeps g8 clear for his Queen), and then the Queen enters 2. Qc8 + ! Qg8 3. Qxc3 + and mate in two.

Smyslov vs. Liberzon

RIGA 1968

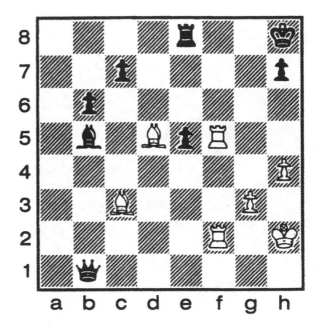

WHITE TO MOVE

KEY: Take center stage

SOLUTION: 1. Rxe5!! and Black resigns. White's battery of Rooks and Bishops insures mate. If 1 . . . Rxe5, then 2. Bxe5 mate. Otherwise, White will move his Rook at e5, giving a thunderous discovered check. A few possibilities: 1 . . . Kg7 2. Rg5+ Kh6 3. Bg7 mate; and 1 . . . h6 2. Re7 mate.

Kotov vs. Smyslov

MOSCOW 1944

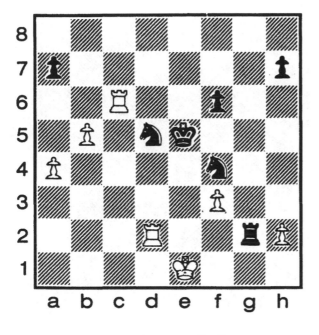

BLACK TO MOVE

KEY: Four easy pieces

SOLUTION: After 1 . . . **Rg1 + !**, White's King is surrounded by a fabric of King, two Knights, and a Rook. The main line goes 2. Kf2 Nh3 + 3. Ke2 Nd-f4 + 4. Ke3 Re1 + 5. Re2 Rxe2 mate.

Smyslov vs. Boleslavsky

MOSCOW—LENINGRAD 1941

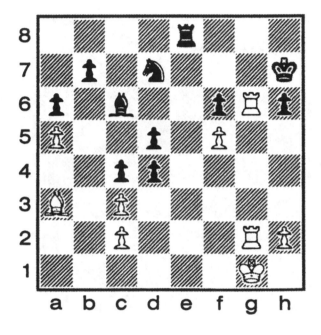

WHITE TO MOVE

KEY: Swing shift

SOLUTION: Decisive was **1. Bc1!**, transferring the Bishop to the other wing. Black resigned, for he couldn't deal with the mate threat at h6 without allowing a two-Rook mate. If 1 . . . Re1+ 2. Kf2 Rxc1, avoiding the mate at h6, then he's still mated by 3. Rg7+ Kh8 4. Rg8+ Kh7 5. R2-h7 mate.

Mikhail Tal (1936-)

WORLD CHAMPION 1960-61
Soviet Union

When Tal captured the title from Botvinnik in 1960, he became the youngest world champion ever up to that point. The games of this dynamic, attacking player have vivid appeal to chess fans everywhere. While still competing in major tournaments and achieving outstanding results, he has also distinguished himself as a journalist and writer. His books and columns are fraught with wonderfully entertaining observations and witticisms.

A violent, elemental force that burst forth on the chess scene in the late 1950s, Tal echoed the attacking proclivities of the great Alekhine. In four explosive years (1957-60), he swept everything before him, ultimately becoming the eighth world champion. A Yugoslavian cartoon of the period caricatures Tal holding a round black bomb with a short burning fuse behind his back. This was his style—an opponent never knew when the bomb would be produced to demolish the position. His games are littered with all manner of sacrifices, combinations, and tactical threats.

Blek vs. Tal

LATVIA 1955

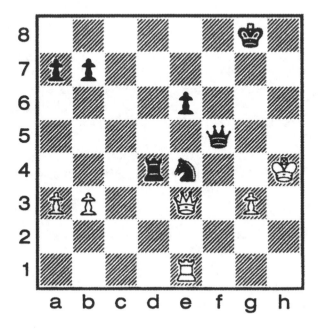

BLACK TO MOVE

KEY: Knightmare

SOLUTION: The winner was the devilish withdrawal **1 . . . Nd2 +** (1 . . . Ng5 also works), which actually led to mate after 2. Qxd4 Nf3!.

Tal vs. Golombek
MUNICH 1958

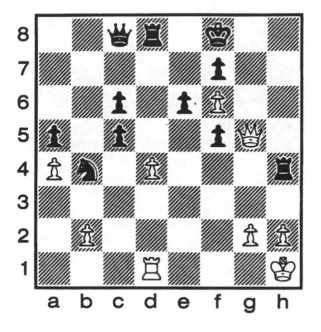

WHITE TO MOVE

KEY: The grand tour de force

SOLUTION: The odyssey began with **1. Qg7+**. The line continues: 1 . . . Ke8 2. Qg8+ Kd7 3. Qxf7+ Kd6 4. Qe7+! (here Black resigned) Kd5 5. Qxc5+ Ke4 6. Qe5 mate!

Tal vs. Ivanovic

BUGOJNO 1984

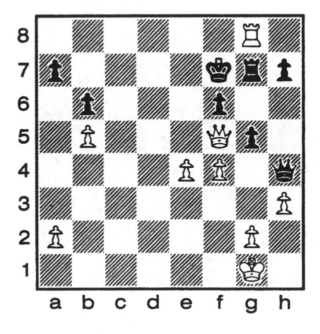

WHITE TO MOVE

KEY: There is nothing like a dame

SOLUTION: So who needs the idling Rook? White's Queen turns on with **1. Qd7 + !**, which soon mates. If 1 . . . Kg6, then 2. Qxg7 + Kh5 3. Qxh7 mate. And if 1 . . . Kxg8, trying to win the Rook, then 2. Qe8 mate!

Tal vs. Calvo

MALAGA 1981

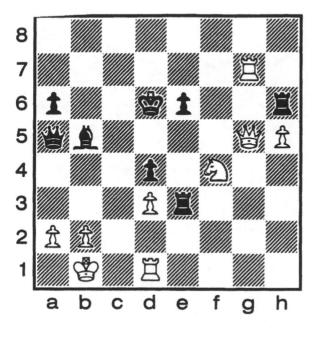

WHITE TO MOVE

KEY: Around the world in five plays

SOLUTION: The circle game went **1. Qe7+** Ke5 2. Qc5+!
Kxf4 (or 2 . . . Kf6) 3. Qg5+ Kf3 4. Qg4+ Kf2 5. Qg2 mate.
And if 1 . . . Kc6, then 2 Rc1+ and White mates fast.

Tal vs. Mascannas

LVOV 1981

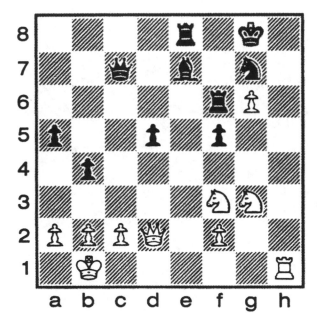

WHITE TO MOVE

KEY: A castle Rooks a King

SOLUTION: White's instant Rook sacrifice mates in four moves: **1. Rh8 + !** Kxh8 2. Qh6 + Kg8 3. Qh7 + Kf8 4. Qh8 mate.

Tal vs. Tringov

AMSTERDAM 1964

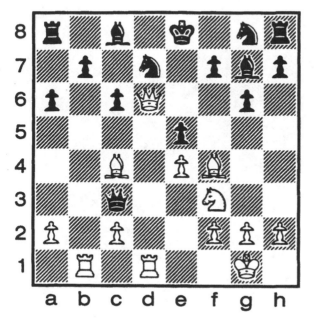

WHITE TO MOVE

KEY: The Bishop looks for a mate?

SOLUTION: 1. Bxf7 + ! Kxf7 (if 1 . . . Kd8 2. Ng5) 2. Ng5 +
Ke8 3. Qe6 + and Black resigned in view of 3 . . . Kd8 4. Nf7 +
Kc7 5. Qd6 mate, and 3 . . . Ne7 4. Qf7 + Kd8 5. Ne6 mate.

Tal vs. Velimirovic
MOSCOW 1977

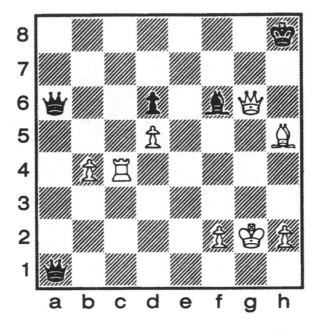

WHITE TO MOVE

KEY: Hey, ladies, check it out

SOLUTION: Black's two Queens must stand by idly and watch the checks after **1. Qh6+**. The game concluded: 1. . . Kg8 2. Rg4+ Bg7 3. Qe6+ Kh8 4. Qe8+ Kh7 5. Bg6+ Kh6 6. Qe3 mate.

Tal vs. Romanishin
TALLIN 1977

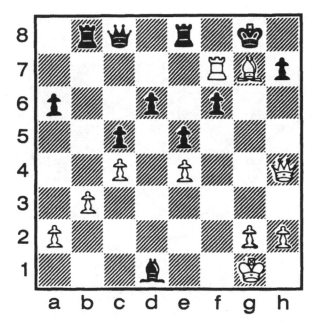

WHITE TO MOVE

KEY: Clear the decks

SOLUTION: The sunburst **1. Bh8!!** opens the 7th rank to White's Queen and Rook. The defensive try 1. . . h5 loses to 2. Qxf6, threatening imminent mate. And no better is 1. . . Kxf7 2. Qxf6+ Kg8 3. Qg7 mate.

Polugaevsky vs. Tal

RIGA 1979

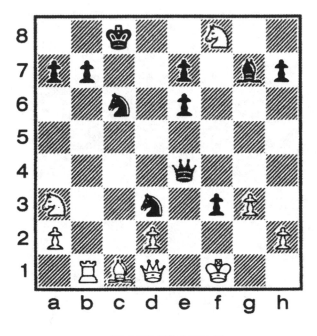

BLACK TO MOVE

KEY: End around

SOLUTION: 1 . . . Qg4! and mate follows. If White tries to avoid 2 . . . Qh3+ by 2. Kg1, then Black mates via 2 . . . Bd4+ 3. Kh1 Nf2+ 4. Kg1 Ne4+! 5. Kh1 Nxg3+ 6. hxg3 Qh3.

Tigran Petrosian (1929-84)

WORLD CHAMPION 1963-69
Soviet Union

One of the least appreciated of world champions, Petrosian's moves often seemed obscure and even irrational. But the logic behind them was almost always there, and indeed for years the accomplished Armenian was an extremely tough man to defeat in a single game. At the time of his death, he was still among the game's highest-rated players.

He earned the nickname "Iron Petrosian" in his early twenties, when he rarely lost a game. Chess to him did not allow guesswork: it was first, last, and always a game of logic in which risks and complications must be avoided. When in the post-mortem analysis of a tournament game his opponent asked, "Why didn't you play this line? It's beautiful and wins by force," Petrosian would reply, "Too complicated. My move also wins and without any fuss." Perhaps his zeal for control hampered his imagination, however, and prevented the attainment of greater heights. Nevertheless, in subordinating his great combinative gifts to the exigencies of tournament competition, he developed into an outstanding position player and a master of the closed game. It was Petrosian whom Bobby Fischer had to overcome in 1971 to earn a shot at the world championship against Boris Spassky. The rest is history.

Petrosian vs. Pachman

BLED 1961

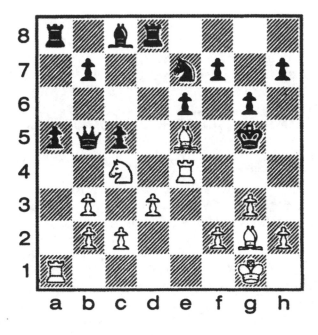

WHITE TO MOVE

KEY: Cut 'em off at the pass

SOLUTION: 1. Bg7! and Black resigned, for his King cannot get back to safety. For example, 1 . . . e5 2. h4+ Kh5 3. Bf3+ Bg4 4. Bxg4 is mate. And so is 1 . . . Nf5 2. f4+ Kg4 3. Ne5+ Kh5 4. Bf3.

Petroslan vs. Pogrebyssky

TIFLIS 1949

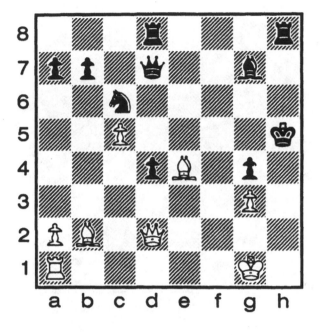

WHITE TO MOVE

KEY: One-upmanship

SOLUTION: 1 Kg2! frees the back rank and threatens the deadly 2. Rh1 mate. Let's see Black try to stop it!

Petrosian vs. Pfeiffer

LEIPZIG 1960

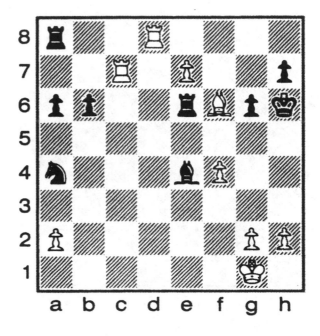

WHITE TO MOVE

KEY: The pawnbroker

SOLUTION: Black resigned after **1. Bg5+**, when the King would be forced up the outer row and thus be at the mercy of White's pawns. If he had tried 1 . . . Kh5 (1 . . . Kg7 walks into a killing discovery), then 2. e8/Q (to unblock the 7th rank) Rxe8 3. h3! wins, for Black cannot cope with both 4. g4 and 4. Rxh7.

Chistiakov vs. Petrosian

MOSCOW 1956

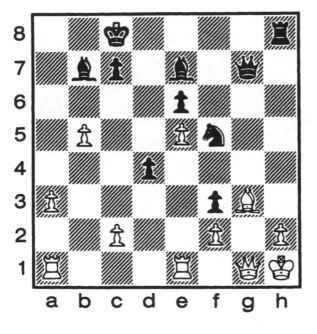

BLACK TO MOVE

KEY: Horse trade

SOLUTION: The simple exchange **1 . . . Nxg3+** compelled White's resignation. It's mate after 2. fxg3 (or 2. Qxg3 Qxg3 3. fxg3 f2+ 4. Re4 Bxe4 mate) 2 . . . Rxh2+ 3. Qxh2 (3. Kxh2 Qh6 mate) 3 . . . f2+ 4. Re4 Bxe4+ 5. Qg2 Qh6 mate.

Petrosian vs. Trifunovic

USSR—YUGOSLAVIA 1959

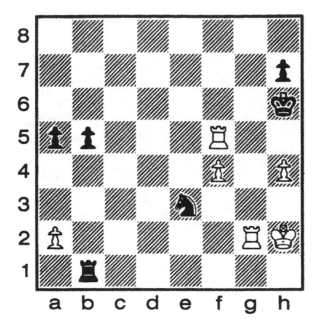

WHITE TO MOVE

KEY: By Rook or by Rook

SOLUTION: The three progressive steps were **1. Rf6 + !** Kh5 (forced) 2. Rg5 + Kxh4 (forced) 3. Rh6 mate.

Tolush vs. Petrosian

MOSCOW 1957

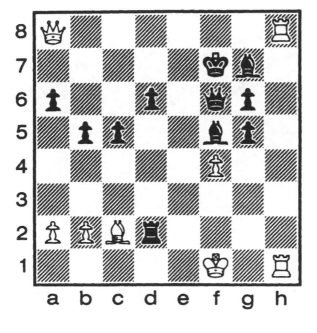

BLACK TO MOVE

KEY: If the check clears, you're in the money

SOLUTION: Tolush threatens Qe8 mate but Petrosian goes first with **1 . . . Bd3 + !,** which unleashes his entire army. If 2. Bxd3, then 2 . . . Qxf4+ and mate follows at f2. Or if 2. Ke1, then 2 . . . Qe7+ 3. Kxd2 Qe2+ 4. Kc1 Qxc2 mate. And if 2. Kg1, then 2 . . . Qd4 mate!

93

Petrosian vs. Stein

MOSCOW 1961

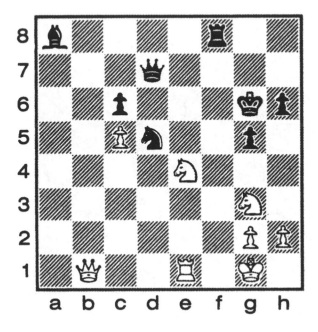

WHITE TO MOVE

KEY: Knights in shining arm-her

SOLUTION: Black resigned after **1. Nf6 + !**, when Black is unable to block with his Rook at f5. Now he loses by either 1 ... Kxf6 2. Nh5 + Kf7 3. Qh7 mate or 1 ... Kf7 2. Qh7 + Kxf6 3. Nh5 mate.

Petrosian vs. Nei

MOSCOW 1960

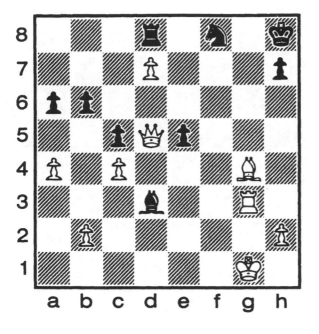

WHITE TO MOVE

KEY: The setup

SOLUTION: With **1. Qg8 + !!**, White creates mate: 1 . . . Kxg8
2. Be6 + Kh8 3. Rg8 mate.

Keres vs. Petrosian

BLED 1959

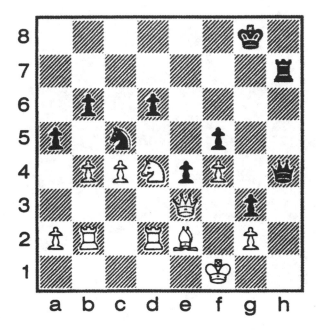

BLACK TO MOVE

KEY: A shot on the dark

SOLUTION: 1 . . . Qxf4 + !! deflects the Queen from the defense of g1 and mates. If 2. Qxf4, then 2 . . . Rh1 mate.

BORIS SPASSKY (1937-)

WORLD CHAMPION 1969-72
Soviet Union

The tenth world champion, Boris Spassky, is known for his brilliantly conducted attacks and over-the-board courage. He played two championship matches with Petrosian, narrowly losing the first by a single game in 1966, and capturing the 1969 match and the crown by two points. For years, he was Bobby Fischer's nemesis, beating the gifted American in three of their first five tournament games (they drew the other two).

In his peak years (1963-69), Spassky's games strongly resembled Lasker's, with a flexible style that he could adjust to suit the opponent. Slashing attacks, sparkling combinations, defensive masterpieces, quiet positional maneuvering, and technical endgames all found a perfect practitioner in Spassky. Some players could handle an individual style better than Spassky, but none could treat all styles at the uniformly high level he attained. He is best remembered for his 1972 championship match with Fischer, the most publicized event in all chess history. Spassky's loss in that competition does not diminish the impact of the most suspenseful games ever witnessed in a summit contest.

Kuznetsov vs. Spassky

KISLOVODSK 1960

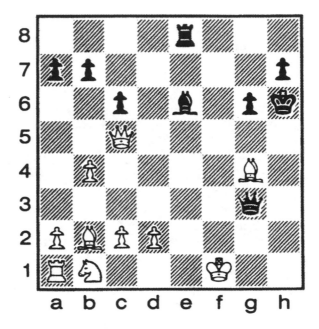

BLACK TO MOVE

KEY: An undercover agent

SOLUTION: 1 . . . **Bc4 + !**, and White resigned, for the released Rook mates next move by 2 . . . Re1.

Vizantiadis vs. Spassky

SIEGEN 1970

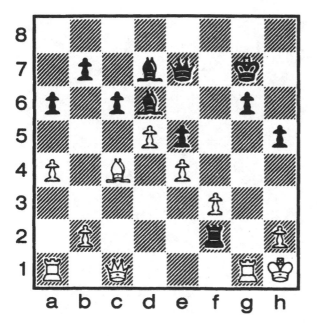

BLACK TO MOVE

KEY: On the take

SOLUTION: The capture 1 . . . **Rxh2 + !** (opening the h-file)
wins after 2. Kxh2 Qh4+ 3. Kg2 Bh3+ 4. Kh2 (or 4. Kh1) Bf1
discovered mate.

Spassky vs. Langeweg

SOCHI 1967

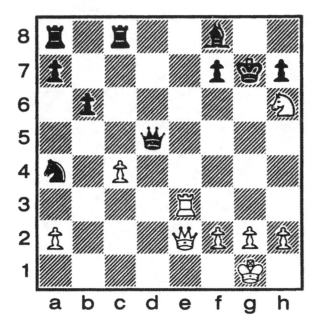

WHITE TO MOVE

KEY: A Knight to remember

SOLUTION: 1. Qg4 + !, and Black concedes. If 1 . . . Kh8, then 2. Qg8 mate. The capture 1 . . . Kxh6 loses to 2. Rh3 + Qh5 3. Rxh5 mate. Finally, 1 . . . Kf6 2. Ng8! is mate, in case you forgot the knight.

Spassky vs. Marszalek

LENINGRAD 1960

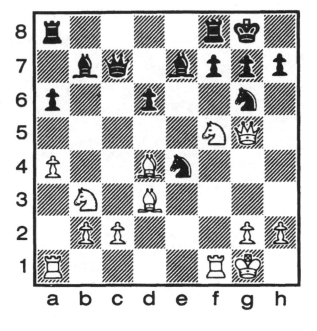

WHITE TO MOVE

KEY: An ounce of intervention

SOLUTION: The Queen squeezes in **1. Qh6!!**, and Black resigns. If 1 . . . gxh6, then 2. Nxh6 mate. Meanwhile, 1 . . . Bf6 leads to like ruin after 2. Bxf6.

2

Spassky vs. Petrosian
MOSCOW 1967

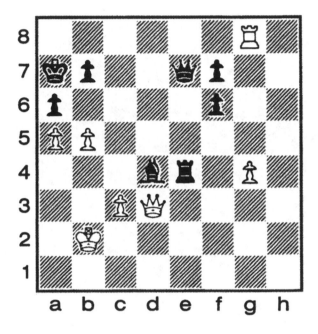

WHITE TO MOVE

KEY: A bolt from the blue

SOLUTION: It's all over after **1. Qxd4 + !**, when 2 . . . Rxd4 allows 2. b6 mate.

Korchnoi vs. Spassky

LENINGRAD 1952

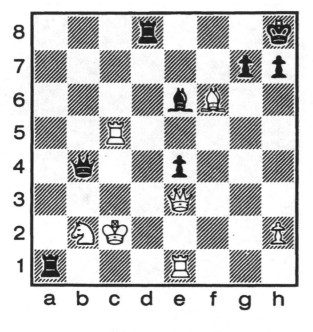

BLACK TO MOVE

KEY: A sacrificial sham

SOLUTION: Once Black forces White to block d2 by the Rook "sacrifice" **1 . . . Rd2 + !** 2. Qxd2, he mates with 2 . . . Qb3. (Equal time for the mates not chosen by Spassky. 1 . . . Bb3 + ! 2. Qxb3 Rd2, or 2 . . . Qd2.)

Bronstein vs. Spassky

RIGA 1967

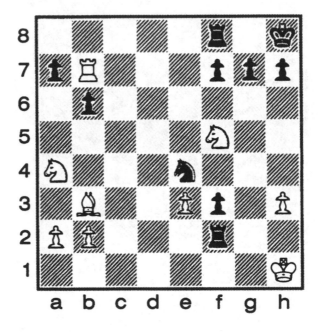

BLACK TO MOVE

KEY: The tender trap

SOLUTION: The quiet, gentle move **1 . . . Rg2!** paralyzes the King and threatens the unstoppable 2 . . . Nf2 mate.

Forintosh vs. Spassky

LENINGRAD 1960

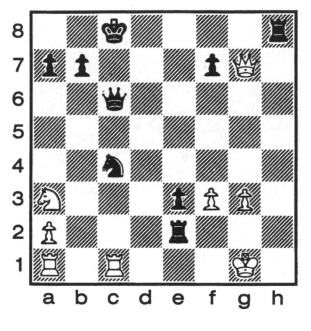

BLACK TO MOVE

KEY: Make him an offer he can't refuse

SOLUTION: The Rook sacrifice **1 . . . Rh1 + !!** forces the King to a vulnerable square and leads to 2. Kxh1 Qxf3+ 3. Kg1 Qg2 mate.

Spassky vs. Korchnoi

LENINGRAD 1968

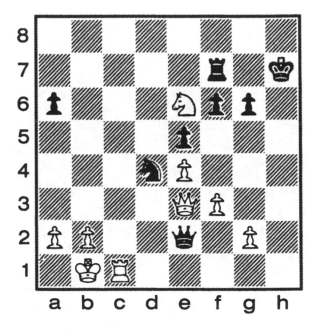

WHITE TO MOVE

KEY: A rude intrusion

SOLUTION: 1. Qh6 + !! and Korchnoi resigned. If 1 . . . Kxh6, then 2. Rh1 is mate. And if 1 . . . Kg8, then 2. Rc8+ Rf8 3. Rxf8 (or Qg7) is mate too.

Bobby Fischer (1943-)

WORLD CHAMPION 1972-75
United States

The highest-rated player in the history of chess (a world chess federation rating of 2780), and the youngest grandmaster ever (15), Robert James (Bobby) Fischer remains an enigma to the chess public. After defeating Boris Spassky in 1972, he failed to defend his title against the 1975 challenger Karpov and lost the championship by default—the only time this has ever happened. Many fans still consider him world champion.

In his boyhood in the mid-1950s Bobby immersed himself in chess literature, becoming intimately familiar with the games of the great champions of the past. He distilled the stylistic essence of these giants and integrated them into his own play. From Steinitz came the passionate search for truth, from Lasker the compelling clash of two opposing wills, from Capablanca the crystalline treatment of the middlegame, from Alekhine the relentless energy poured into every contest, and from Euwe and Botvinnik the scholarly approach to opening research. Stylistically, Fischer is closest to the 1930s champion, Max Euwe, who was eulogized by Alekhine as never making a tactical mistake in conducting an attack. This description of perfection applies equally well to Fischer, for Fischer has made fewer tactical errors than any other world champion. Indeed, this is the key to his success, overriding and coloring every aspect of his play. An eminent rationalist, he prefers a simple, straightforward strategy, and only Fisher among all modern masters has the prescience to implement such deceptive schemes.

Larsen vs. Fischer

DENVER 1971

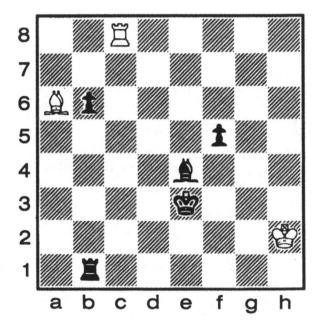

BLACK TO MOVE

KEY: Back track

SOLUTION: The slight retreat **1 . . . Kf4!** triumphs, for White cannot stop Rh1 mate.

Fischer vs. Panno

BUENOS AIRES 1970

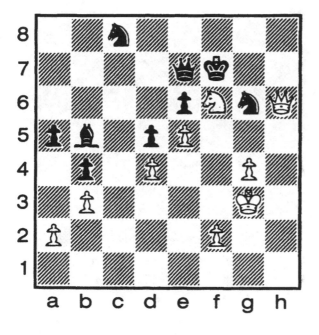

WHITE TO MOVE

KEY: Two-timing Queen

SOLUTION: The Queen "checks in" twice and mates **1. Qh7+** Kf8 2. Qg8.

Denker vs. Fischer

NEW YORK 1959-60

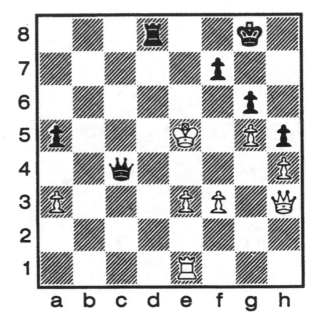

BLACK TO MOVE

KEY: Up the ladder of distress

SOLUTION: 1 . . . Rd5 + forced resignation, in that 2. Kf6 Qc6 + 3. Ke7 Qd6 + 4. Ke8 Qd8 is mate (4 . . . Qf8 is also mate).

Bisguier vs. Fischer

NEW YORK 1965-66

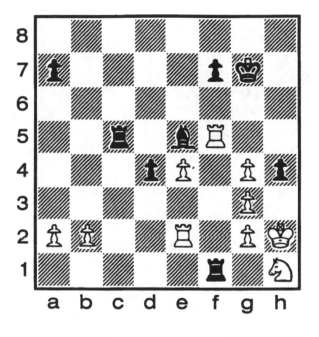

BLACK TO MOVE

KEY: Drawn and cornered

SOLUTION: The King is driven to mate after **1 . . . Rxh1 + !** 2.
Kxh1 Rc1 + 3. Kh2 Bxg3 + (or 3 . . . hxg3 +) 4. Kh3 Rh1 mate.

Fischer vs. Kupper

ZURICH 1959

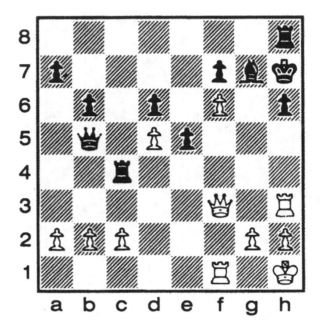

WHITE TO MOVE

KEY: An interference pattern

SOLUTION: By checking first before taking the Bishop, White forces the enemy King to obstruct his own Rook. After **1. Qf5 + !**, Black must answer 1 . . . Kg8 allowing 2. fxg7 and subsequent mate.

Greenblatt Computer Program vs. Fischer

CAMBRIDGE, MASS. 1978

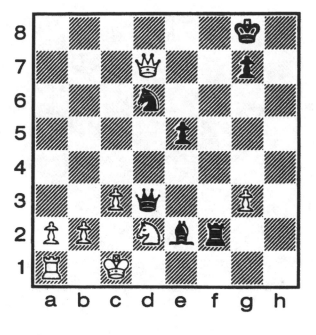

BLACK TO MOVE

KEY: A Knight deposit at the bank

SOLUTION: The d-file is cleared by luring the Knight to the back rank with **1 . . . Rf1 +** 2. Nxf1 Qd1 mate.

Doda vs. Fischer

HAVANA 1965

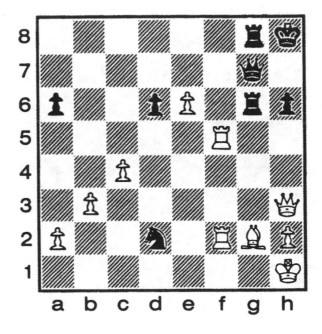

BLACK TO MOVE

KEY: The long arm of the law

SOLUTION: 1 . . . Qa1 + ! leads to mate. If 2. Rf1 (2. Bf1 Rg1 mate) 2 . . . Nxf1, and Black threatens the homicidal 3 . . . Ng3, a discovered mate.

Fischer vs. Weinberger

MILWAUKEE 1957

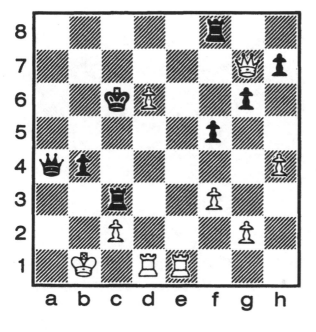

WHITE TO MOVE

KEY: Ring around the King

SOLUTION: White's major pieces encircle Black with **1. Qc7 +**, when 1 . . . Kb5 2. Qb7 + Kc5 (2 . . . Ka5 3. Rd5 + with mate next move; and if 2 . . . Kc4, then 3. Qd5 mate) 3. Re5 + Kc4 4. Qd5 mate. The central square d5 is the focal point in each of the three finales.

D. Byrne vs. Fischer

NEW YORK 1956

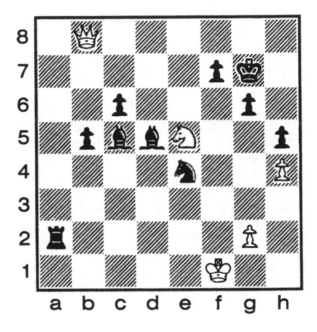

BLACK TO MOVE

KEY: The roamin' army

SOLUTION: The famous conclusion to the "Game of the Century" went **1 . . . Ng3+** 2. Ke1 Bb4+ 3. Kd1 Bb3+ 4. Kc1 Ne2+ 5. Kb1 Nc3+ 6. Kc1 Rc2 mate (it's also mate after 6 . . . Ba3). The harmony of Black's four attacking pieces is striking.

Anatoly Karpov (1951-)

WORLD CHAMPION 1975-
Soviet Union

Anatoly Karpov, the twelfth world champion, is the only contender to have assumed the title without having beaten the previous champion even in a single game. He was given the top spot in 1975 when Bobby Fischer refused to play because of a rules dispute with the world chess federation. There will always be doubt over the outcome of "the match that never was," but in every other sense Karpov has performed as a great champion, including two successful title defenses (Baguio 1978 and Merano 1981) against arch-rival Viktor Korchnoi.

With his intuitively fine feel for position play, Karpov fits neatly into the Capablanca-Smyslov camp. Like the legendary Cuban, Karpov possesses a well-developed sense of danger that allows him to keep the opponent at a distance. Like Capablanca, too, Karpov exhibits tremendous confidence and sits down at the board with total assurance of victory. Botvinnik has defined Karpov's recurrent theme as domination. No matter how well the opponent's pieces appear to be placed at a given moment, Karpov eventually drives them back, leaving the field open to his own forces. Too bad this technique cannot be learned, for it could move chess theory a gargantuan step forward. Apparently, it's an intuitive process that not even Karpov can explain.

Karpov vs. Zoldos

HUNGARY 1973

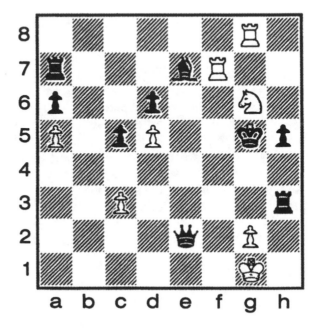

WHITE TO MOVE

KEY: Here a horse, there a horse, everywhere a . . .

SOLUTION: White's Knight nicely coordinates the two Rooks:
1. Nxe7 + Kh4 2. Nf5 mate. If 1 . . . Kh6, then mate by either
2. Rg6 or Nf5.

Karpov vs. Pomar

NICE 1974

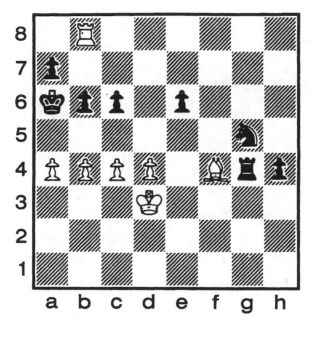

8 7 6 5 4 3 2 1
a b c d e f g h

WHITE TO MOVE

KEY: Preparation B

SOLUTION: With the preparatory Bishop move **1. Bd2!**, White veils an attack against a5 and threatens the advance 2. b5+, with subsequent mate. If 1 . . . Rg3+, then 2. Kc2 b5 3. cxb5+ cxb5 4. axb5 mate.

Karpov vs. Mecking

HASTINGS 1972-73

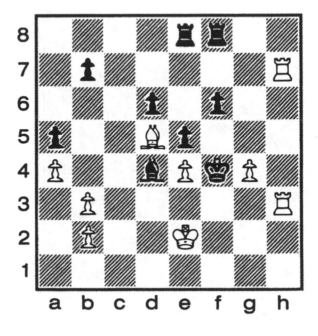

WHITE TO MOVE

KEY: Castles in the air?

SOLUTION: The subtle cutoff **1. Rg7!** forced Black's resignation, there being no way to avert 2. Rf3 mate. A beautiful handling of the Rooks.

Karpov vs. Talmanov

LENINGRAD 1972

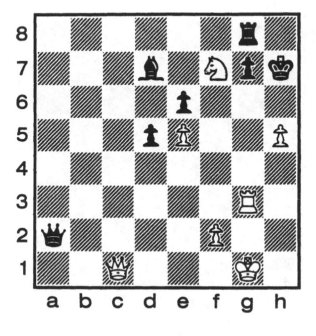

WHITE TO MOVE

KEY: Double trouble

SOLUTION: By doubling his major pieces on the g-file, White constructs a mating net: **1. Qg5!** Qb1+ **2. Kh2** and Black resigned. If 2 . . . g6, then 3. Qh6 mate; and if instead 2 . . . Be8, then 3. Qg6+ Qxg6 4. hxg6 is also mate.

Karpov vs. Robert Byrne

HASTINGS 1971-72

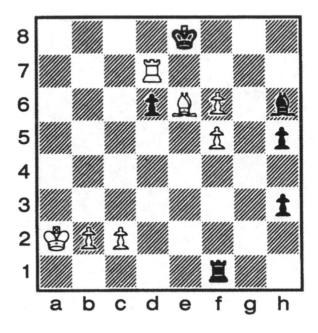

WHITE TO MOVE

KEY: Sail the high C's

SOLUTION: White's control of the c-file leads to mate after **1. Rc7!**, when Rc8 is in the offing.

Karpov vs. Sax

LINARES 1983

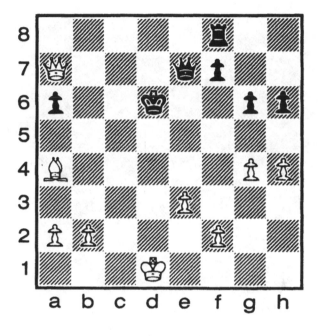

WHITE TO MOVE

KEY: Distant assistant

SOLUTION: The Queen sets it up **1. Qb6+!** Ke5 2. Qd4+ Ke6. But the Bishop applies the finishing touch from across the board with 3. Bb3 mate!

Torre vs. Karpov

TILBURG 1982

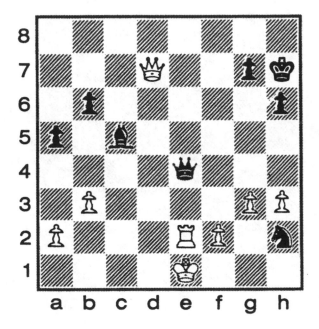

BLACK TO MOVE

KEY: At cross purposes

SOLUTION: The diagonal check 1 . . . **Bb4+** mates next move. If 2. Kd1 (or Qd2), then 2 . . . Qb1 is mate.

Karpov vs. Najdorf

MAR DEL PLATA 1982

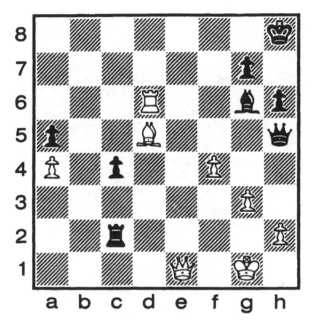

WHITE TO MOVE

KEY: A Bishop blocked is the Queen's quest

SOLUTION: The winning move is **1. Rd8 +**, and in the main line White maneuvers to obstruct Black's Bishop: 1 . . . Kh7 2. Bg8+ Kh8 3. Bf7+ Kh7 4. Rh8+ Kxh8 5. Qe8+ Kh7 6. Qg8 mate. Of course Black also loses if he tries 1 . . . Be8, for 2. Rxe8+ Kh7 3. Bg8+ Kg6 (or 3 . . . Kh8 and he's mated as before) 4. Qe6 is mate.

Korchnoi vs. Karpov
BAGUIO 1978

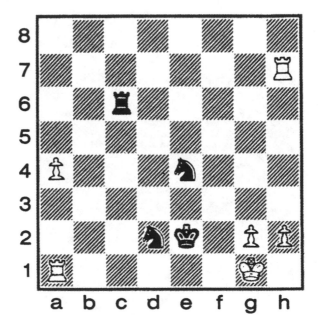

BLACK TO MOVE

KEY: Knight time

SOLUTION: The galloping coda was **1 . . . Nf3 + !**, and White resigned. If 2. gxf3, then 2 . . . Rg6+ 3. Kh1 Nf2 mate. And if instead 2. Kh1, then 2 . . . Nf2 mates at once.

About the Author

Bruce Pandolfini, a U.S. National Chess Master, gained prominence as an analyst on PBS's live telecast of the Fischer-Spassky championship match in 1972. In due course, he lectured widely on chess and in 1978 was chosen to deliver the Bobby Fischer Chess Lectures at the University of Alabama in Birmingham. His first book, *Let's Play Chess*, appeared in 1980. The author is a *Chess Life* magazine consulting editor, for which he writes the monthly "ABCs of Chess." He has also written columns for *Time-Video*, the *Litchfield County Times*, and *Physician's Travel and Meeting Guide*.

As a chess teacher, he's been on the faculty of the New School for Social Research since 1973, and currently conducts chess classes at Browning, Trinity, and the Little Red School House in New York City. With U.S. Champion Lev Alburt, he has developed special children's programs sponsored by the American Chess Foundation. The director of the world famous Manhattan Chess Club at Carnegie Hall, Pandolfini visited the USSR in the fall of 1984 to study their teaching methods and observe the controversial championship match between Anatoly Karpov and Gary Kasparov.